MISCARRIAGE
OF A DREAM

MISCARRIAGE OF A DREAM

In Pursuit of Purpose

REGYNA COOPER

MISCARRIAGE OF A DREAM

By Regyna Cooper

© Copyright 2014 by Regyna Cooper
Maxser Publishing
P.O. Box 20147
Towson, Maryland 21284
www.regynacooper.com

Library of Congress Cataloging-in-Publication Data
Cooper, Regyna Annette Cole (Regyna Annette Cole Cooper), 1968- . Miscarriage of a Dream/
Regyna Annette Cole Cooper.—1st ed p.cm.
Summary: Overcoming how things may appear to experiencing a dream becoming reality.
ISBN 978-0-9844667-2-6
Personal Development- Motivation & Inspiration.

ISBN: 978-0-9844667-2-6

PRINTED IN THE UNITED STATES OF AMERICA

ACKNOWLEDGEMENTS

God, thank you for whispering so many gifts to me before I was in my mother's womb; I am thankful that Jesus went to the cross and rose for me to have access; and to the Holy Spirit for reminding me and guiding me along this journey.

My husband, James R. Cooper, for reminding me how to dream big. Your love, support, friendship, and guidance have been a blessing. You are my greatest dream come true.

My son, Andrew J. Cooper, for reminding me how to believe in the impossible. I love you and I love watching your growth both physically and spiritually.

My mother, B. Mae Allen, for showing me how to enjoy the moments when they arrive. May God continue to bless you in the newest season of your life as Mrs. Rose. Thanks Mr. Leroy Rose for helping to keep her smiling.

To my brother, George F. Allen; sister, Alisa Allen; and God-sister, Ann-Marie Champ, for being true to what Daddy (George Allen) always taught by example. "Be truthful and honest with yourself and with others, and you will walk a life of success."

Debi Caldwell only God can reunite sisters and give them the blessing of becoming great friends.

To Rachel Orovio – Thank you for being an angel in my life.

To Pastor Cheryl Hill for being a pathway to helping me discover the importance of knowing God intimately for myself.

To Glen Tabron and Carlene Cole…thank you for pushing me to be great, especially when I didn't see it for myself.

Love to my family and close friends. Your support gives me strength.

In memory of my family members who paved the way for me through prayers and by example in life.

The future belongs to those who believe in the beauty of their dreams. ~Eleanor Roosevelt

My dream is to be successful in all God has planned for me. Some may say that is a bit vague. Ralph Waldo Emerson says the following about success:

> *Success is to laugh often and much, to win the respect of intelligent people and the affection of children. To earn the appreciation of honest critics and endure the betrayal of false friends, to appreciate beauty, to find the best in others! To leave the world a bit better, whether by a healthy child, a garden patch or a redeemed social condition. To know even one life has breathed easier because you have learned to live in your purpose. This is to have success.*

Is my dream vague?

No. It is big enough to allow God to be God in my life.

CONTENTS

FORWARD

Dream Carrier: A person who is created to assist you to see your dreams come true.

Regyna Cooper is the ultimate dream carrier.

Much like the midwives who care for mothers today, there is a need for people with specialized training to help us with our unrealized dreams. This is training that cannot be learned in a classroom. These skills are acquired through the pain of their own delayed dreams, of having a heart full of compassion and a passion to see another person succeed in their God given purpose. This describes Regyna to a T. How do I know? As her husband, friend and business partner I have seen up close and personally the mountains Regyna has climbed. I have seen her put her own dreams on hold to help birth the dreams of another. I have seen her unbridled passion as she fiercely defends the dreams of another. I have seen her laugh publicly but cry alone as she questioned God about why her dreams had not manifested, yet held onto the belief that our God is able and will do what He has promised. And most importantly I have had the privilege of witnessing Regyna's own birthing, to see her realize her purpose, to see her megawatt smile as she recognized her greatness; in a word to see her dreams come alive.

This book is the outcome of many hours of study, prayer, tears, pain and laughter. All of these were required to get to the essence of your biggest problem; why haven't MY dreams come true? Regyna will guide you through the ups and downs to recognizing you in your pursuit of your dreams, of realizing how God and you will come together to see the work completed. Prepare yourself for the ultimate rollercoaster ride; your life begins again now!

It is my honor to introduce the love of my life Regyna Cooper to the world. May you read and learn from here examples. May your life be brightened by her experiences. May you receive the blessings of the Lord as you open your mind to the reality of what is to come. Like the Apostle John, we wish that you prosper and be in good health, even as your soul prospers.

James R. Cooper

Pastor, Author, Success Strategist

INTRODUCTION

"There shall be no one miscarrying or barren in your land..."
Exodus 23:26 NAS

This book was birthed out of seeking an answer to what could have been perceived by many as a loss of a dream. The difference is this wasn't a wishful dream. This was a dream God had placed in my spirit and one He had me holding onto for years. In the midst of the pain and shock of loss, was something my mind and flesh could not comprehend. There was an unsettling and a sense of peace all at the same time. In other words, I was right where God wanted me. Even with the support of my husband and family, my strength had to come from the Lord. The journey of knowing me begins with a glimmer of understanding the depth of God's love for me; shown through every dream received, deferred and realized.

(●————DREAM RECEIVED,
DREAM DEFERRED,
DREAM REALIZED ————●)

A true dream is a vision, thought, or idea that is so tangible it causes a change in one's physical and/or mental condition. This reaction does not come from hearing, seeing, or hoping for a dream belonging to someone else. Your dreams are the dreams that impact your life personally and directly. So much that you find yourself preparing and expecting them to occur.

What happens along the way to this vision, is self-discovery and the accomplishment of more than you could have ever imagined.

Miscarriage of a Dream

How I view and understand my dreams have changed greatly throughout my life. I have learned much and continue to gain more understanding daily. Our dreams are more than wishful thinking. When there is a passing thought, which keeps passing and won't leave our heart, it is something to note.

I have always had a mothering heart.

When I married there was not a question in my mind of if I would become a mother, rather it was more a question of when it would be the most convenient in our lives.

To our surprise, God put a prayer on my heart to pray for the health and safety of a relative and the child she was carrying. I had no thoughts that this child would be an answer to a dream. In our minds we were still not in a place to be ready to have a child. So an even greater surprise, the child I had been praying for in the womb, became our first. He is still a blessing and has taught me much about myself and what is possible.

Through the years, I have had the pleasure of birthing and mothering businesses ventures. Some were successful and others did not develop as expected. Through the processes I learned what should and could happen, and had to understand that some things were outside of my control. I learned the impact of miscarrying, misplacing, and mishandling dreams. With the loss of businesses, I questioned why but never to the extent of the why of losing a child.

In the aftermath of the miscarriage of our next child; I, a woman of faith, had to honestly pause and ask to see the bigger purpose than the one I was feeling at that moment. There was never any doubt that God loved me, however there was the question of why. Please understand, this was not the first loss I had ever experienced in my life. Loved ones had passed, and to a lesser extent, business opportunities I thought were going bring me wealth died before my eyes. These business ventures were babies I poured time, passion, and money into for an expected outcome. However, the promise of this child was one of those promises and desires that I had shared with many. So why would God allow this to be a part of my journey? The interesting thing is in that moment, I did not have the thought that I would not carry healthy children. I knew this particular promise and gift was mine. My husband and I had already been blessed with raising a wonderful and powerful son who is full of life. But the understanding of what God was telling me and what direction He was leading in that moment was cloudy. So the question I needed an answer to was, "What does miscarriage mean?"

Definition of Miscarriage:

> [1.] *The expulsion of a fetus from the womb before it is able to survive independently, esp. spontaneously or as the result of accident.*

> [2.] *An unsuccessful outcome of something planned: "the miscarriage of the project".*

When I looked it up, I expected the first definition, but the second definition is the one that stood out. "An unsuccessful outcome of something planned." We have all found ourselves in this situation at one time or another. If you think about it, it is probably relatively easy to think of five such situations from your own experiences. Whether it is a child, job, business, home, or family; when we have walked something out and the outcome was not as successful as expected, it is a miscarriage, and we feel a loss.

Has there ever been a moment in your life when you just knew something you have been working, fighting, hoping, dreaming, and holding onto was upon you so strong you were beginning to see the evidence of it happening? You were filled with excitement and anticipation. Now, there was still a chance everything would not work out as planned, but in your heart you are saying "I know this is for me." It may have been closing a big project in business, purchasing your dream home, seeing a family member you never thought you would see again coming home, or a long awaited pregnancy and birth. This list can go on and on, but when the events unfold in ways you didn't expect or want, the overwhelming feeling which instantly comes upon you is hurt and missed opportunity. The next question is "Why?" (you can find yourself stuck in this place for a varied period of time). My prayer is that your time in this place lasts no longer than necessary. Next, is how do you move forward? This is when we come to the crossroad. Do we keep looking at the situation we see with our natural eyes or do we trust what we know to be true in our heart of hearts? Do we lose hope and become frustrated, or do we continue to hold onto the victory within our reach? This is a place of knowing that you know. Believe me; I know it is hard to know when everything you can see or speak seems impossible. Thank God, He has given us the power and provision to do the impossible. He said you can do all things through Christ. That means with God, your situations change from impossible to I'm possible with Christ.

Enjoy the journey of discovering you as you go through the process.

Dream Received

"WOW!!!" That is the first thought and response to seeing, imagining, or hearing what could be possible. Then our thoughts quickly go to "But who am I to do or have this?" The next question is "How will this even be possible?"

Walk Not By Sight ——————●)

You have a vision, a dream, or a thought about your future, which you cannot shake. You are excited. You wonder if it could actually happen. You may even be thinking, how it could happen. Then the perception of what you think needs to be done hits, and those huge leaps into the possible become fear steps held down with weights. You keep thinking you need to see it clearer to go one more step. But in order to get to your destination, you have to make the first gesture and lean into your future.

How do you lean into your destiny when you are not sure where you are going? First, you have to trust the word of the Lord and decide to run straight into your destiny. This could be referred to as running through.

Many times we see something that excites and motivates us to get started on a project, plan, design, book, song, or whatever is placed on our heart. We start with the mind-sight of reaching the goal. At some point we look up and the goal appears to be further than we originally thought. Next, every step begins to feel heavier and harder to achieve. This is the place where our mind-sight must stay focused on the direction of the goal. I said direction, instead of the goal itself, intentionally. So many times we stop because the way seems to be blurred. Our vision and the target don't appear to be as clear and sharp to our sight any more. But if you keep moving in the original direction, you will keep getting closer and will have gone further than you may have thought possible.

A few years ago, I had the pleasure and joy of running a 5K. Let me give you a bit of background on this run and how it relates to me. Less than a year prior to the race, I recall having a conversation with a friend, stating that running had to be one of the worse things to do. I said I would rather walk fast, than beat my body up by pounding my feet on the hard pavement. A few months later another friend, Mom Strategist Mia Redrick, asked me about running a 5k with a group of women. I laughed it off and said, "It's a walk/run correct?" Walking distances had never been a problem for me. So when she said yes, I figured that would be my way of supporting the team, walk the race out.

As time got closer, maybe three months or so out, I started seeing ads and hearing people talking about this little race I had signed up for with this group. One lady told me about all these people who had been training for this event over the past few months. When I inquired more, she said there are women in their sixties who are just leaving people in their dust. Now, I am beginning to realize that I had not been taking this serious enough. So I said to myself, "Ok, I am going to start walking my neighborhood." I would map out a distance of 5 kilometers (a little over 3 miles) with my car and then walk it out to figure out the distance I had agreed to run. Well I can say that the first day took me about ninety minutes to cover this distance. Not knowing what I should expect, I was pretty satisfied. Again, I ran into someone talking about this race and they are talking times

(●———IF YOU KEEP MOVING IN THE ORIGINAL DIRECTION, YOU WILL KEEP GETTING CLOSER AND WILL HAVE GONE FURTHER THAN YOU MAY HAVE THOUGHT POSSIBLE. ———●)

of thirty minutes. Hold everything! Do you mean I am that slow? I am going to have these sixty year old women flying past me? Leave it to the Lord to work on your pride and fitness all at once!

At this point I realize - it's a set up by the Lord. So I have learned when the Lord gives you something, say "Thank You" and give it back to Him for guidance on how to execute the plan. So that is exactly what I did. With my whole heart I decided I wanted to see what was possible. The Holy Spirit became my personal trainer. I was committed to getting up and out the door to run every day, but I asked for guidance as soon as I walked out of my door. True to form, the first week I was out walking and a gentleman who had to be in his mid-seventies was walking a distance behind me. I remember turning a corner and halfway down the block this man had made up a huge distance on me. Next thing I know the man is passing me! I couldn't believe it. All I heard within me was this, "His pace is your minimum pace; you must not drop below that pace." I watched and picked up the cadence of his steps and that rhythm stayed with me. I never caught up to that man again during that walk, but I did keep pace. Every day I started with walking, running and listening. One morning, about a month before the race, I started as usual. I showed up and said, "Ok Lord, what are we doing today?" This particular day, He sent me on an entirely new route and it was full of hills. I kept saying to myself, "I should go back. This is too far." Yet I kept hearing, "Trust Me." That was the day I learned you should not always look at what is to come. Sometimes you just have to look right in front of you; only seeing the place you will step next. When you walk up a hill and only focus on the next step, the slope is not perceived to be as steep to your mind as it really is. So your mind does not have the opportunity to rationalize how painful the incline should feel. Your body still feels the burn, but it does not have time to anticipate how much it should naturally hurt. I did not look up until I felt a release to do so. By that time I realized, I was close enough to the top that I didn't want to give up. What a feeling it was to get to the top. I finished my walk that day in one hour. I was feeling confident that I would not be the last to cross the finish line anymore.

Here is the next catch to this run. I never really paid attention to the day of the race. I knew the date, but assumed it was on a Saturday. To my surprise the race was on Sunday at 8am. This cannot be possible. God has had me training for this race and now I will not be able to make it. My husband and I lead a ministry from our home every Sunday morning, starting with prayer at 10:30am. So I was thinking it will be impossible to run this race, get back to the car (which is parked about 3 miles away from the race course), drive thirty minutes home, get cleaned up, dressed and ready for prayer on time.

That night the Lord whispered, "You are going to run." I didn't know whether to smile or cry, so again I simply said "Ok."

When the day of the race arrived. I was ready to go and meet the group. All I heard in my spirit was "It's you and Me." By the time I parked, picked up my race number and packet, I could not find the group of moms I planned to join, in the crowd of thousands. Again, this was my first race ever. I was excited and nervous. The race was about to start and I heard, "You are going to do this in 45 minutes." I thought about that for a second and then as the words sank in I suddenly blurted out loud "WHAT?!!" The race began and I started running with everyone. This pace was a little fast, but I was feeling good. I was sticking to it and then I ran into the physical brick wall of my body saying, "What are you doing?" I could not run another step, but through it all I could see the cadence of the older gentleman, from the neighborhood, in my mind and I couldn't fall below that pace. I caught my breath and started running again. As I ran, I started focusing on the light poles. I would run to one and say "I'm still alive. I can make another." When I couldn't run, I kept the pace.

I was about two-thirds through the race. I had no watch, so I did not know my time. I had walked more than I thought I should, but I was still moving. I turned a corner and thought I would see the finish line, but it was not there. It was on the other side of the harbor and I could feel my body saying to me, "I'm almost out of steam." God always sends what you need right when you need it. Right at that point I heard a woman encouraging her friend. She said, "We can do it. We are almost at 45 minutes." Still at my pace, I asked, "What did you say?" She repeated, "We are almost at 45 minutes." I don't know how I must have looked, but that was all I needed. I recalled the words the Lord spoke to me at the beginning of the race, "You will complete this race in 45 minutes." It was as if I were running a hundred yard dash. I ran with everything in me towards that finish line. I crossed in a little over 46 minutes. Did I make my goal of completing a 5K? Yes. I ran the race, made it home and was dressed before the first person arrived.

That's when I realized my goal of running the race was too small. The experience was an opportunity to develop a deeper relationship with God. The true goal will always be a part of who I am. I now have a knowing of what all things are possible with Christ really means. This can only happen, when you are not walking by sight, but trusting Him.

Fear is to be Overcome ─────●)

Fear, we think of it as such an ugly word. It is something we all have experienced at one time or another; and at various levels. Fear can paralyze, but it is also the catalyst to learning our true strength. Please understand that on a spectrum, fear and faith (hope) are diametrically opposed (both are the substance of things not seen; one is for your good the other is not). However, if you never know one, you can never fully experience the other. Everyone is born into this world with a limited fear instinct. Studies have shown that all babies are born with two fears: one is the fear of falling and the other is the fear of loud noises. Fear has limited power, but it is real to us. On the other spectrum we are taught to have the faith the size of a mustard seed and childlike faith. Although they are both part of us, they do not operate or exist together. So why are we born with any fear at all.

Discovering the depth of our faith comes from overcoming fear when it is necessary to move forward. David, for example, being real, had to have a bit of fear in the midst of the indignation which propelled him to face Goliath. If we never had any fear, how would we learn to overcome and to trust that there are better situations and circumstances ahead?

Every fear learned from our human experiences must be overcome to achieve greatness. To build the Empire State Building during the Great Depression, climbing Mount Everest, stepping onto the Moon, opening a business, leaving home for college, getting married, walking by faith, all require us to stop hearing what is spoken around us and hear only the truth. At the end of the day, God gives us a choice in all we do. When you decide to step out of the boat into your greatness, you have to know your focus in order to stay steady.

The ability to overcome is a direct result of the conviction which created the fear and the determination to see the situation differently. That may sound strange, however, there has to be a belief in place to allow a fear to take root. The only way to destroy the fear completely is to discover the source and overcome it at the point of the root. This can be something you say to yourself without even realizing; such as I will never fly on an airplane. This thought usually comes because there is no understanding of the physics of flight. Does this mean you have to have a degree in physics to overcome the fear? Or do you have to have a faith in something greater than the fear created by the thought of flying? Most would agree it to be the latter. Let's pose this question: If the fear never became realized, would you have any reason to acknowledge anything greater to overcome the situation? My Great-aunt Edith once told me she could only fly if she imagined God's hand carrying the plane in the air and landing it at the destination. As one of the first in her family to fly, she overcame by knowing God was much greater than anything she could fear from a plane.

This may sound like an oversimplification of a situation. However, when you put fear in its place, all things are possible. Faith and hope will allow you to walk through storms, because it comes with wisdom. Walking with faith, hope and wisdom gives you the boldness needed to impact your family, friends, community, country and the world. That's what faith can do. So all the sayings are true; fear must be overcome. It is overcome with a focus of truth, transparency and genuine faith, which makes all things possible.

Nice to Meet Me ─────●)

In walking through and overcoming, we come to a place where we need to know ourselves to move forward in our true purpose. Through this process we learn what is possible. We can also discover our true aspirations and inspiration. Dreams which are easily let go or altered, in most likelihood, were thoughts and ideas picked up from others in the first place. For example, a singer has someone tell him "You are so gifted. I can see you in front of thousands on stage." Having the ability to sing is a blessing. Being in the business of singing can be draining, if your true dream is to teach music. This also goes for dreams easily achieved. If you are blessed to walk quickly into your desire, but once there realize there is still emptiness; maybe this was a part of a larger vision or somewhere you were positioned to be for the service to someone else. It would not be considered your dream fulfilled. This occurs in families all the time. A relative has a dream she speaks of often. Maybe she wants to be a business owner, however during her youth, it was difficult to access the finances needed. Fast forward she sees an opportunity and keeps speaking of how important it is to own your own. Because this is a person you respect and you know you want to be your own boss, you pick up the baton. The problem occurs when you find you have rushed into something and realize this is not particularly the type of business you wanted. While everyone around is excited about your launching, the only thought coming to your mind is "How long is this going to last?"

So, what's next? Reevaluation and reflection are the next steps. When you start hearing things over and over from people near and far, it is time to start paying attention. But when do you know when to act. Many times we accept things as truth because we keep hearing it mentioned. If we check, we may find the idea is coming from people within the same sphere of influence. Learn to seek guidance for yourself. Learn to understand how God communicates with you. Pray, fast, sit still, and hear. All of these are keys to understanding who you are, and most importantly, providing the reflection to know how these desires and aspirations fit into your purpose.

The journey of meeting you begins with being honest with yourself and with others about your true self. Sometimes we have worn a mask for so long we don't even realize that one is being worn. Sometimes we have to go through an event that pushes us so far out of the comfort zone of the mask, that there is a type of reboot that occurs. Just like a computer, a reboot does not erase the hard drive; it gets rid of the glitch which may have caused slow performance.

You have a choice. You can go back to doing the same thing and going to the same places you did before the reboot; or you can seize the opportunity to run with greater power and performance into the purpose you were originally created for. Remember, all the data picked up and housed prior to the reboot and needed for your destiny, is still in place. But, all the junk has been shaken off. So the most important difference is the way you respond to inquiries. Some things should be dealt with swiftly, and never completely downloaded into your hard drive. Knowing the difference is the beginning of being self-aware and empowered to say what is acceptable in your life.

Miscarriage of a Dream

Dream Deferred

What happens when that thing you can see, is so clear in your mind that you can describe it in detail, yet it still has not arrived. You wait and you wait. You look around and you see it happening for others. People keep agreeing with you, that they know it is going to happen for you, but still nothing. This can cause the strongest belief to be shaken.
So how do you make it through?

(●————Viability…Get Better, not Bitter

What is going on when everything looks like it is going as planned and then we get a curve ball thrown our way? Things begin to unravel, fall apart and may even appear dead. How can this be possible? We received, believed it could be possible and started seeing what we perceived to be the promise coming to pass. The first thing we do is wonder what happened or what we did wrong. Then the blame game starts. We point at ourselves, others, and even God.

The strangest part is the desire to birth this dream has not diminished, even with all the pain. It has not been reprogrammed for you to let go. It is your promise from before you were born, according to chapter 29 and verse 11 of Jeremiah. We want to push on and need to push on, but there is a voice saying, "Maybe this isn't for you." This is not the time to give up. If the dreams and desires are pulling at you, then there is still a pulse and rhythm of a promise deep within you fighting to be birthed. This may sound strange, but let us walk this out.

The hardest thing to hear is that your dream, as you believed it to be, is not viable. What is being said? You can see it and almost physically feel it, but for some reason it is not sustainable. Why would God allow you to get so close, only to pull you back?

The last thing any of us wants to hear is that we were not ready. How do you better prepare for something you have been waiting for and anticipating for months or even years? What more can you do? You pray and fast and people are still saying, "You are not in a place of receiving." This is the place where we should post a giant red stop sign. This is the place where we should stand still. Dr. Seuss called this the waiting place in his book "Oh, The Places You'll Go". The problem is getting stuck in this place. When we wait, we should only be waiting on God's direction; for God to be our personal guide. This is the time to clear our minds off of all the reasons we can't and the baggage of fear. Remove the voice of people who swell your head up and those pulling you down. Both of these extremes work on the emotions of ego and pride. The only emotion God participates with us in is love.

Once we have cleared our minds in honesty and transparency, we can come to a place where we are ready to move in the flow of the Lord and receive His instruction. The other thing we need to understand is there is a time and season for our dreams and promises to occur. Ecclesiastes 3:1 teaches, *"to everything there is a season, and a time to every purpose under the heaven"* (KJV). This is not simply the purpose of life, but the purpose for everything we accomplished in this life.

Before we start doing all we can, to be all we can be in our own strength, inquire of the Lord. Ask Him the purpose and the season for the dream He placed on your heart. There is a song which says, "...after you done all you can, you just stand". We stand in the hope

(●————————THE ONLY EMOTION GOD PARTICIPATES WITH US IN IS LOVE. ————●)

and trust. Understand the word is standing "in" not "on". Standing on leaves your hope open to outside sources. Standing in, is fully submerged in the confirmed promise of the Lord. All dreams given of the Lord will come to pass and be an inheritance as promised. Understanding and believing that according to Philippians 1:6, *" being confident of this, that He who began a good work in you will carry it on to completion until the day of Christ Jesus."*

Viability is not based on what we see with our natural eye or on what any person says through a prophetic word. Viability comes from knowing; believing and having faith in all God has promised you. Become confident in the strength God has given you to press through in Him. You are His child and He will build and prepare you to birth everything He has promised.

A child is not viable until the sperm and the egg have an encounter. This is no simple task. Let's think about this journey. The sperm that makes it through had an alliance of protectors and an inner program design for its purpose. That sperm is going to live its purpose or die in the effort. There is no other recourse. When it was released, it was released with a design imprint. When the mission was accomplished, you were created. If it took all of this to get you here, you have been released to accomplish exactly what you were created to do. Your imprinted dreams are written on your heart to propel you into your purpose.

Is your dream viable? The fact that we are here today, means your purpose is viable, it means you have purpose and destiny, because the sperm and egg destined to create you came into contact and made your life, purpose and dreams viable. As mentioned in chapter 3, these are your God given dreams to your specific purpose. If your first attempt does not come out as planned, try again. If your finances or health doesn't look as if it is favorable to your promise, focus on God and all He has spoken to you.

Shaken, Not Stir Crazy ———●)

In the midst of walking things out we can experience feelings which could make us feel like we are completely losing our minds. Nothing seems right. Even the simple things do not appear to be getting accomplished. Stop and take a deep breath. No, really stop. It is all for our good. That statement even sounds strange. We can think of this as a shaking off period. It is a time when some old things, which have been held on to for too long start falling away. It is a shake and not a stir. This is a very important distinction. When things are stirred they simply get blended together. Sometimes they dissolve, but most things can still be easily identified when stirred. Our natural senses want to figure out all the components of the mixture. We could have the tendency of wanting to say I know what it takes to do this myself. When things are shaken, things fall off and fall out. You may even see where things have fallen, but they are not to be picked up again. When everything settles down after the shaking, you may notice things appear to be everywhere. Things may be on the floor and even broken, so what do you do? You examine what is left and how it was left. Was your glass so full that nothing else could fit until some things were shaken out? Were there pictures on your shelf, which no longer had significance? Were there beliefs from your childhood which no longer apply for where God is taking you? Sometimes we need an earthquake in our lives to get us to where God wants us.

The truth of it all is that we need to have the human reality shaken off of us; the realities and thoughts we have received from television, friends and even family. Much of these are presented without any harm intended. The problem is the filter for delivery or even our state of mind when receiving is based off of hurt, challenges, disappointments, wrong timing, or all the above.

Don't be upset by the disruption or what appears to be a mess. There are few people who may be in your life, for your entire life. We have to learn to be led by God for those who should stay and those who should go. There is a staleness, which can turn toxic when people remain longer than their particular season. Some people are designed to come in and out of our lives multiple times. This provides strengthening for everyone. The disciples were a perfect example. They were sent out in groups to share the gospel, but would come back together from time to time and go again in the same or different sets. Always recognize what the Lord is doing in your life. Don't be bitter. Just know the Lord is pushing you into the new and into a sweeter season. Don't worry. Things that need to be gone are simply being shaken off, and you learn that the weight of the journey is the Lord's. He is our true support system when walking into destiny.

Experience is a Factor, Not Time ●)

Have you heard this before, "You haven't been praying enough" or "You have to spend more time with God" or "You have to learn to pray correctly"? There always seems to be a person in your life, who is repeatedly telling us we are not doing enough. And it hurts ten times more when it comes from a Christian. It hurts worse because they are singing a tune we have all heard before. The song that says you're a sinner and will never be good enough, the song of you're not giving your best, the song the world has programmed into your mind, the song we sing to ourselves; that we will never be worthy. The song of the accuser.

Let me help with this right now. No one is worthy. That is why Jesus went to the cross for each and every one of us. We are as filthy rags, but for the blood of Jesus. Make no mistake about it. Our righteousness was paid for with a price, this is the foundation of our salvation. So don't let anyone tell you, you are not good enough. Simply say I know, but Jesus is worthy. Jesus is worthy of every dream God has given me to fulfill; the destiny and purpose for which we were specifically designed. God is not a respecter of man and age is not a factor. We should look for the fruit. God will send wisdom to direct in love, patience to correct in love and our obedience is built from the very same love. Love doesn't hurt, but is remembered for the freedom it brings. If you always feel a weight when you leave someone's presence or worry about their instruction more than the Lord's, there is a problem.

The next question is usually, "How do I know when it is God?" In the world, and in church, a common saying is "Something told me." The Holy Spirit has many names, but "something" is not one of them.

Test the spirits, just as it says in 1 John 4:1. Ask that voice you are hearing,

> *"Do you know Jesus who went to the cross for my sins, do*
> *you know the one who took the power of death and the*
> *grave, do you know the one who sits at my Father's right*
> *hands and intercedes on my behalf?"*

If you hear no response, do not follow the unction or direction of that spirit. Cast it out on the name of Jesus, so there may be no more hesitation or distractions. You will begin to hear clearly and recognize the voice of our Father. Trust what He is telling you is perfect for you and for the time in which He is calling.

Time is precious and can be lost, but time is not a limiting factor in achievement. A wise man by the name of Bill Bailey once said, time is a system created by man....if you want to become an expert quickly, start putting yourself in situations to increase your experience or that will get you to where you want to go. No one knows the exact time in which all elements of a specific occurrence are going to take place. Something may be scheduled, but no one will be able to predict the exact weather conditions for the moment in that space, except God. When you trust that God has it all under control, you can run full force into experience. Create and look for opportunities to serve. Be available to share love and grace. You will find when walking according to God's plan you look back and have no idea how you were able to get so much accomplished, in what seemed to be a short time. That is how God's time works. He makes the way and there is no way for us to fully understand, except He gives revelation.

Miscarriage of a Dream

Dream Realized

There was a woman with a desire to accomplish something she figured was out of reach because of her age. When she tried to do things too early and without guidance she got a result that didn't produced the outcome she expected. After she experienced a few things and became comfortable with herself, things came with ease and worked out just as planned.

Missed Outcome,
While Searching For The Prize ———————●)

We have all had those moments. Trying to get to a destination and you drive right past the street you needed because of a distraction. Whether it is a great conversation with a passenger, thinking of where you have to be in the next hour or the project you left on your desk at work. Whatever it may have been, you drive right by the entrance or road you needed.

It is interesting how things can be missed in the chase. You may even give up wondering if it is really worth the time. However, when in pursuit of something, deterrents are ignored. You figure out how to overcome the obstacle. You grow patient waiting for the right moment to move. Frustration and fear are no longer your friends, simply because you do not have the time to entertain them. It is all about the pursuit.

Blessings may be missed or given away, as Esau found out. Dreams may be deferred, Joseph is the perfect example. But God's promises are His commitments and He will assure they will come to pass. The Bible is full of God's promises to His people. Did you ever stop to see the pursuit that was a part of each one? Noah had to build an ark for a downpour of something he had never seen. Think of what his neighbors were saying about him. Mary had to deal with the gossip of being an unmarried pregnant woman. Moses had to deal with a community of people who kept giving up on God. Abram must have heard his friend say he was crazy to think he was going to be the father of anything. There are many other examples; however the pursuit of God's purpose was all the same.

Too many times we get caught up on what we did in the past. In many biblical accounts, the people questioned whether God had the right person. People hid and some ran from the call of God on their lives. But God didn't stop his pursuit of them. Jonah is the perfect example of this scenario. God gave him a word to share. Jonah decided he was going to jump on a fishing boat going in the total opposite direction. God disturbed the waters so much that Jonah had to go overboard into the ocean. He was so stubborn it took days in the belly of a whale to get himself together. When they accepted what God said about them as truth, their destinies changed. Their pursuits moved them into greater power and authority.

The way may not be clear to us all the time, but know that God's promises do not return void. What He begins, He will complete. Dream big and stand steadfast in God's Promises.

(●————Recognize When You Have Arrived

People say, "I'm not going to miss my blessing!" What does that mean? If it is your blessing how could you possibly miss it? Others may say, "I'm waiting on my blessing!" The question is how long should you wait and are you in the right place? Is it possible God is waiting for us to move into position for our blessing? If God had instructed many of us to go to the brook as He told Elijah, we would have had ravens circling around waiting for us to pick a place that was comfortable enough for us to get settled. Think about a brook. Vocabulary.com defines it as a natural stream of water smaller than a river. This would not flow as wide or as far as a river, but for most of us, making that decision on the brook would have been overwhelming. The decision could have been so overwhelming that we would have not noticed the ravens waiting for us to rest. I can even see myself at times seeing the ravens with my natural eye and not recalling how God said they would serve me because of being so preoccupied with where to stop. A raven is recognized as one of the most intelligent birds. It is also seen as a scavenger that does not discriminate between humans and animals. During this time of drought, my mind would have probably assumed these birds were waiting for me to die. So as long as I was moving I would live. Right?

Miscarriage of a Dream

Many times our blessing is right in the hands of what causes us fear and stress. If your blessing came in the mouth of what appears to be an enemy, would it be accepted? It is time for us to move, receive and respond based on the promises of God. Too many of us are waiting for the Hollywood flashing lights to let us know we have arrived.

When we start to appreciate the process, the present, the now, and enjoy the journey, we discover we have arrived. God is I am. He is the same yesterday, today, and forever. This is truth. It is also true that God does not live in our yesterday and tomorrow is not promised. That would mean God's focus is on our now. If God has already mapped out our lives, why would He be concerned about if we are going to make our destination? He makes the path straight. We, in our free will, go about our lives complicating things. We must recognize and celebrate God in this very moment. This moment determines the next, but as soon as this moment passes, we have the ability to change our trajectory. No matter the path we take, as long as our faith and our salvation are in the Lord, we win.

My prayer is that I get this understanding more quickly each day; and that by doing so I am eliminating the wasted time of worrying if I am getting this whole life journey correct. When I am in synch with God's will and purpose, nothing can take away the dreams God has given me. When we get to a place of peace in the promises, whether they appear good or unfavorable, we are finally recognizing the very essence of the peace of our Lord. So how do we know when we are in pace and hearing from God? Keep a journal of your dreams and what you have inquired of the Lord. Be patient and wait for confirmation. In faith and belief the answers will come. You will understand more and more the purpose of the dream in your life. Some dreams are instant miracles that are great; however as Joyce Meyers once said "The quick ones don't usually build character." Some dreams are faith builders. When they come to pass, our relationship has grown in patience, faith and trust. Some dreams are not realized as anticipated, but they are just as sweet, because you learn that God has you through it all and the road you have taken in pursuit has taken you further than you could have ever imagined. This is a place of deeper understanding and revelation of Hebrews 11:1 *"Now faith is the substance of things hoped for, the evidence of things not seen."* Right now is the time we start receiving the blessing of our dreams, and all God intended of our dreams. Dreams achieved are checkpoints along our journey to purpose. They are confirmation that we are on the right path. Dreams deferred are not penalties, as some suggest. God is not holding up blessings to punish anyone for sin. Jesus paid the price for all our sin. He didn't skip or miss any. God will protect us, so we don't find ourselves overwhelmed. So again, the key is to live in our now and celebrate what God has placed in our hands. Knowing *"that in all things, God works for the good of those who love Him, who have been called according to His purpose"* Romans 8:28.

(●————— Coming to Pass

Keep moving forward. There's more to come. Once your dream has become a reality keep pressing forward. There will be times when you want to turn back, because we don't like to associate our dreams with any level of frustration. You have to know there is always some. There will be people who don't understand and sometimes there are just natural pains in the process. The pass occurred to helps us understand how much we can handle. No matter how painful it gets, it has gotten you to this point. You are right where you belong for this now-moment.

Coming to pass does not mean the end. Just as a dream deferred is not a dream denied. The demise of a dream only occurs when you allow it to die. Some say you can grow too old for a dream to come to pass, but the truth is only you can define what your dream means to you. A dream was never meant to hold you captive and be kept hidden from the world. Your dream is to give you endless hope and fill you with possibility. Even when everything seems to go against you, your dream breathes life in you again. Your dream should help you see lands you only imagined and accomplish more than your mind could fathom. You see, your dreams allow you to burst through the shell the world will build around you. Each dream is a breath of fresh air. Our dreams are the inspiration that reveal our love of ourselves. The love of what God has created us to be. For truly there is no limit to God's love. We decided how far and how deep we will allow it to reach. Can dreams miscarry or be aborted? Yes, if you let them go, they can; but the impression and direction they cause us to take cannot be denied. Moses did not enter the promised land with the children of Israel. However, he and Elijah appeared when Jesus transformed on the high mountain (many believe the mountain was Mt. Tabor), which is in lower Galilee. If this is the case, Moses was in the promised land with Elijah and Jesus. Abraham is the father of many nations. It came to pass, but did he see it? Or by faith did he see what was to come to pass? We all have dreams. To act as if you never had a dream is to stop the beauty of a breath. Try it; take a deep breath right now. No matter where you are in the world, you have just experienced your environment in ways some will never be able to comprehend. That breath whether good or bad just made an imprint that will cause you to want to experience it again or wish you had not been in that particular circumstance. Either way you can't erase it. So what do you do with it? If enjoyable, soak it all up; experience every detail so you can share the very essence of the moment. If you thought you were in a good spot only to realize the aroma was not as pleasant as the view or things appearing to your eyes are misleading, you still have just had an experience you can share. Knowledge and wisdom of a situation you can now pass on to others. It is only a waste if you walk away in disgust, without a thing learned.

I have learned much along this journey. Dreams miscarried, aborted, distorted and fulfilled. Through it all my dreams have pushed me to speak before crowds, travel to lands I had only imagined and most of all learn to be grateful for whom I am created to be right at this moment. Tomorrow my list of dreams and possibilities may change and grow, but I will always know the source of my hopes and dreams that can never be denied. That is what makes life genuine, a breath worth taking and a dream worth reaching.

Miscarriage of a Dream

Dreamer – Carrier

Now that you have an understanding of your dream, you may be asking,
"How do I carry it out?" You may have begun to notice you are
running into many people with good hearts who want to help,
but you have to know your dream carriers.

Your Assigned Dream Carrier ──────●)

As mentioned previously, you have to know who is assigned to help you birth your dreams. Each dream may have a different person to get them to the needed position. There may even be several people overlapping or one who is there from beginning to end. The most important step in identifying these people and discerning who is in position is prayer.

God has blessed me with the ability to help people carry dreams, without the desire to claim them as my own. This is a key principal and a warning. Any person who tries to take ownership or credit or becomes envious of the dreamer is out of order for this particular position. They may be great supporters in other areas, but not in carrying the dream.

(●──────THIS IS ALL ABOUT MOVING WITH GOD. ──────●)

Trying to force-fit people into our puzzle only leads to frustration. Trust that God knew what He was doing when He outlined a triangle and created the circle to fit elsewhere. When a leader is needed to motivate, encourage and challenge you forward, that is who will provide support to press in. When assistance is needed because there are too many things to handle at one time, it will be provided.

I am blessed to be a person, who helps people carry out their dreams. The journey to understanding this gift was the answer to a dream and prayer as well. How do you know if you have the grace needed? I would not presume to understand the greatness of God and how He does what He does, but I will share with you the basics of the formula God has shared with me.

The traits God has sharpened in me along my journey are patience, understanding, wisdom, compassion, and determination. The person with the dream has to know this dream is God given. If there is any question, please review the earlier chapters before moving forward. This is all about moving with God. As a dream carrier, the role is to go to God and ask if this is a field in which you are to serve. One of the obstacles to avoid is walking in your own strength. When this occurs, you will find the bumps along the road will quickly lead to a derailment instead of obstructions overcome to achieve victory.

(●————————Going the Distance

The process of carrying a dream is commitment, visualization, organization, and action. The dreamer has the passion while the carrier is committed to the assignment. Please understand, you can be a dreamer and a carrier, but usually not on the same assignment. Yes, we must encourage ourselves in the Lord always. So we are always carrying and leaning forward with our dreams into God. For this conversation, we must understand who we are. In either role we have to be comfortable going to God and being honest. He already knows our thoughts and is just waiting on us to trust that He does know all and His plans are good. So as you journal your dreams and where He wants you to help, ask God what and who you need along the journey and write down what you hear. Watch God move in the subtle and grand gestures. Through it all give God the glory. This is how we become prosperous, even as our souls prosper.

FINAL NOTE

Know that the work has begun. One of the interesting things I have discovered along this journey is that the work to follow a dream is not in our efforts. The work is learning to trust God; not in words, but in all things. This is where dying to our flesh and being led by the Holy Spirit is the building of our relationship with our Heavenly Father. The path to achieving dreams is a journey. Our dreams were never meant to define who we are in this life. Our dreams are designed to enhance our journey and act as stepping stones to purpose. Along the way, there may be bumps, mishaps, missed steps, and even misunderstandings of directions. Through it all, they give us testimonies of tests overcome to share the glory of God. When the understanding of our journey is received, held onto in the longest of nights and become realized, there are no miscarriages. There are only opportunities for God to deepen His relationship with us and introduce us to who He created us to be.

Embrace the process and enjoy the journey. Use the following pages as your personal faith file. Write down those dreams God has written on your heart. Be patient with yourself and with God. His timing is perfect. The word says in 2 Corinthians 12:10, "...*for when I am weak, then I am strong*". Your dreams are not miscarried as long as you don't let them go. Our strength comes from the one who is the author and finisher of our faith. Write the promises He has you holding onto. And note the journey. Learn to celebrate the highs and lows. "*Give thanks in everything, for this is God's will for you in Christ Jesus.*" (1 Thessalonians 5:18 HCSB).

To learn more or ask any questions visit me at
www.RegynaCooper.com

How to Use the Dream Journal

The purpose of the Dream/Promises Journal is to document your conversations with God. As you read this book and gain more clarity to the dreams God placed in your heart, capture them immediately. The book is not designed to give you all the answers; however it is design to prompt you to open your hands and receive what God has for you. To recognize those things God has given to you to spread and share with others. We all share every day. It is up to you whether the seed you sow will cause weeds or flowers to grow.

Each week write what God is telling you and how He used you to be a blessing that week. As you start to review, you will discover the power of walking in your destiny and God-given purpose.

Dreams/Promises Journal

Week 1:

_____

_____

_____

_____

_____

_____

_____

_____

_____

_____

_____

Week 2:

_____

_____

_____

_____

_____

_____

_____

_____

_____

_____

_____

Week 3:

_____

_____

_____

_____

_____

_____

_____

_____

_____

Week 4:

_____

_____

_____

_____

_____

_____

_____

_____

_____

Miscarriage of a Dream

Week 5:

_____

_____

_____

_____

_____

_____

_____

_____

_____

_____

Week 6:

_____

_____

_____

_____

_____

_____

_____

_____

_____

_____

Week 7:

_____

_____

_____

_____

_____

_____

_____

_____

_____

_____

Week 8:

_____

_____

_____

_____

_____

_____

_____

_____

_____

_____

Miscarriage of a Dream

Week 9:

_____

_____

_____

_____

_____

_____

_____

_____

_____

_____

Week 10:

_____

_____

_____

_____

_____

_____

_____

_____

_____

_____

Week 11:

_____

_____

_____

_____

_____

_____

_____

_____

_____

_____

_____

_____

Week 12:

_____

_____

_____

_____

_____

_____

_____

_____

_____

_____

_____

Miscarriage of a Dream

Week 13:

_____
_____
_____
_____
_____
_____
_____
_____
_____
_____

Week 14:

_____
_____
_____
_____
_____
_____
_____
_____
_____
_____
_____

Week 15:

_____

_____

_____

_____

_____

_____

_____

_____

_____

_____

Week 16:

_____

_____

_____

_____

_____

_____

_____

_____

_____

_____

Miscarriage of a Dream

Week 17:

_____

_____

_____

_____

_____

_____

_____

_____

_____

_____

Week 18:

_____

_____

_____

_____

_____

_____

_____

_____

_____

_____

Week 19:

_____

_____

_____

_____

_____

_____

_____

_____

_____

_____

Week 20:

_____

_____

_____

_____

_____

_____

_____

_____

_____

_____

Miscarriage of a Dream

Week 21:

_____
_____
_____
_____
_____
_____
_____
_____
_____
_____
_____

Week 22:

_____
_____
_____
_____
_____
_____
_____
_____
_____
_____
_____
_____

Week 23:

_____

_____

_____

_____

_____

_____

_____

_____

_____

_____

Week 24:

_____

_____

_____

_____

_____

_____

_____

_____

_____

_____

Miscarriage of a Dream

Week 25:

_____

_____

_____

_____

_____

_____

_____

_____

_____

_____

_____

Week 26:

_____

_____

_____

_____

_____

_____

_____

_____

_____

_____

_____

Week 27:

_____

_____

_____

_____

_____

_____

_____

_____

_____

_____

_____

Week 28:

_____

_____

_____

_____

_____

_____

_____

_____

_____

_____

_____

Miscarriage of a Dream

Week 29:

_____

_____

_____

_____

_____

_____

_____

_____

_____

_____

_____

Week 30:

_____

_____

_____

_____

_____

_____

_____

_____

_____

_____

_____

Week 31:

_____

_____

_____

_____

_____

_____

_____

_____

_____

_____

_____

Week 32:

_____

_____

_____

_____

_____

_____

_____

_____

_____

_____

_____

Miscarriage of a Dream

Week 33:

_____

_____

_____

_____

_____

_____

_____

_____

_____

_____

_____

_____

Week 34:

_____

_____

_____

_____

_____

_____

_____

_____

_____

_____

_____

Week 35:

_____

_____

_____

_____

_____

_____

_____

_____

_____

_____

_____

Week 36:

_____

_____

_____

_____

_____

_____

_____

_____

_____

_____

_____

Miscarriage of a Dream

Week 37:

_____

_____

_____

_____

_____

_____

_____

_____

_____

_____

_____

Week 38:

_____

_____

_____

_____

_____

_____

_____

_____

_____

_____

_____

Week 39:

_____

_____

_____

_____

_____

_____

_____

_____

_____

_____

_____

Week 40:

_____

_____

_____

_____

_____

_____

_____

_____

_____

_____

_____

Miscarriage of a Dream

Week 41:

_____

_____

_____

_____

_____

_____

_____

_____

_____

_____

_____

Week 42:

_____

_____

_____

_____

_____

_____

_____

_____

_____

_____

_____

Week 43:

_____
_____
_____
_____
_____
_____
_____
_____
_____
_____

Week 44:

_____
_____
_____
_____
_____
_____
_____
_____
_____
_____

Miscarriage of a Dream

Week 45:

_____
_____
_____
_____
_____
_____
_____
_____
_____
_____

Week 46:

_____
_____
_____
_____
_____
_____
_____
_____
_____
_____

Week 47:

_____
_____
_____
_____
_____
_____
_____
_____
_____
_____

Week 48:

_____
_____
_____
_____
_____
_____
_____
_____
_____
_____

Miscarriage of a Dream

Week 49:

_____

_____

_____

_____

_____

_____

_____

_____

_____

_____

Week 50:

_____

_____

_____

_____

_____

_____

_____

_____

_____

_____

Week 51:

_____

_____

_____

_____

_____

_____

_____

_____

_____

Week 52:

_____

_____

_____

_____

_____

_____

_____

_____

_____

Bonus Gift and Notes and Thoughts

There are songs that inspire us to push forward. I want to share two of those songs with you. The first is *Butterfly Beautiful* by Pastor Tanya Blount Trotter and the other is *Dream Chasers* by Pastor Michael Trotter, Jr. Both of these songs were written by my dear friend and brother in the spirit Pastor Michael Trotter, Jr. I am sharing these to inspire you to keep on dreaming. People may have counted you out, but you still have a dream. You still have breath. Let your dreams keep giving you a fresh breath of life to chase your purpose. Even those not birthed as imaged have an impact. We must protect our dreams. To allow them to be killed by ourselves and kidnapped by those who have crossed our paths is a travesty. You have everything needed to see your dreams birthed. As per the words of *Dream Chasers*, "Don't let go." Thanks Michael and Tanya for sharing your God-given gifts with the world. I truly love you both.

To hear the songs and receive updates and inspirational notes, become a member of the Walking into Destiny family at www.RegynaCooper.com . It's a movement for NOW.

Regyna Cooper is CEO of Maxser Consulting Group, LLC, Licensed Life and Health Insurance producer, Publisher of From Crackers to Caviar, published author in the Amazon bestselling book The Queens' Legacy and author of Miscarriage of a Dream, and Purpose Coach. Regyna is Co-Pastor of Restoration International Christian Ministries in Towson, Maryland. She and her husband James R. Cooper are philanthropists who lend their support to non-profits, organizations and individuals with time, money, and resources privately as God leads. This very diverse resume also includes a background in Event Planning, Strategic Planning, Auditing, Management Reporting and Budgeting with several of the country's largest banking institutions. This has given her a wonderful perspective to reference when providing solutions and multiplying all God puts in her hands.

To contact Regyna Cooper visit www.RegynaCooper.com or email maxser@maxsergroup.com

Miscarriage of a Dream

www.ingramcontent.com/pod-product-compliance
Lightning Source LLC
Chambersburg PA
CBHW052217090426
42741CB00010B/2575